SCHOLASTIC'S A+ JUNIOR GUIDE TO GIVING A SPEECH

SCHOLASTIC'S A+ JUNIOR GUIDE TO GIVING A SPEECH

LOUISE COLLIGAN

SCHOLASTIC INC.
New York Toronto London Auckland Sydney

ISBN 0-590-42147-6

12 11 10 9 8 7 6 5 4 3 2   0 1 2 3 4/9

Printed in the U.S.A.   28

First Scholastic printing, August 1989

Table of Contents

1: Speech! Speech!
   Where Do I Start?....................... 1

2: Card Tricks:
   Developing and Organizing
   Note Cards 21

3: Speakeasy:
   Practicing and Delivering
   Your Speech............................ 40

4: Speaking of You:
   An Informative Speech 51

5: Speaking of Social Studies:
   A Narrative Speech 66

6: Speaking of Opinions:
   A Persuasive Speech 81

Index 103

1
Speech! Speech!
Where Do I Start?

Did you know that most people would rather see an insect crawling on their plates than speak before an audience? Believe it or not, year after year, surveys show that the all-time, number-one fear grown-ups have isn't getting attacked by giant spiders, but giving a speech!*

If you are looking for a way to keep from turning into one of those people who would rather get stuck in an elevator than give a talk, or face a snarling dog rather than an audience, then this book will help.

As you read these pages and follow the advice, you will discover that delivering a speech is like a lot of other jobs you do. It involves simple steps that you can tackle one at a time. This book will show you how to take teacher-sized subjects and

---

* *The Book of Lists*, David Wallechinsky, Irving Wallace, and Amy Wallace.

turn them into kid-sized ones. You will find out how to organize your thoughts so that you'll remember them. This book will show you how to get and keep your audience's attention. You'll learn what to do if you forget what you were going to say. And you'll discover some special cures for the jitters. Finally, you will see just how all of these suggestions work out in three sample speeches.

Whether you have to give a talk about a hobby, an oral report for social studies, or a campaign speech for student council, the steps will always be the same. What's even better is that these steps will work for the short, simple speeches you have to give in middle school now *and* come in handy in the older grades.

No matter what kind of speech you have to give, the following steps will help you do a super job.

10 Steps to A+ Speeches

Step 1: Make up a schedule to prepare your speech.

Step 2: Decide what you are going to talk about.

Step 3: Take notes on your subject.

Step 4: Decide on the purpose of your speech.

Step 5: Organize your notes according to the purpose of your speech.

Step 6: Recopy your note cards for the middle of your speech.

Step 7: Write out your opening and closing sentences.

Step 8: Try out your speech and make any needed changes.

Step 9: Practice the final version of your speech.

Step 10: Deliver your speech.

Step 1: Make up a schedule to prepare your speech.

Imagine that you've heard the dreaded words: "A week from today I would like everyone to deliver a speech to the class." Before you start wondering whether or not you can work up a case of the chicken pox by then, here's what to do.

Find out what you are supposed to do.
First, listen carefully to your teacher's directions about the assignment. Write down anything that sounds important. Put any handout sheets you get straight into your notebook. Before class is over, make sure you know the answers to the following questions:

• What subject am I supposed to talk about?

• Do I have to tell my teacher exactly what I'm going to talk about?

• How long is my speech supposed to be? (Most classroom speeches are three to five minutes long.)

• What is the due date of my speech?

• Am I supposed to write my speech out on paper, use note cards, or memorize the whole speech?

• Do you think there will be a snow day the day my speech is due?

You probably won't get an answer to the last question, but when you finish this book, you won't need any excuses to get out of giving your speech, either!

Once you have your due date, make up a schedule for getting your speech done. This is where an important tip about speech-giving comes in: THE BEST WAY TO CALM THE JITTERS IS TO BE PREPARED. And the best way to prepare is to work on your speech a little each day to get comfortable with it.

Budget your time.

Let's say your speech is due in a week. Here's how to budget 15 to 20 minutes a day:

• Give yourself a couple of days to think about your speech and get information on it. Visit the library if you need to look up information you can't get anywhere else.

• Spend some of your regular homework time one night to take notes and decide on the purpose of your speech.

• Schedule one night to arrange your notes in

the order of your speech. Write out the first and last paragraphs of your speech.

• On the last two nights, try out your speech by reading right from your notes. Make any changes in your speech. Spend the remaining time practicing your final version for about ten minutes in front of a mirror, with a tape recorder, or with another person.

Why not cram all this into one night and get it over with? Well, think about what happens to your body when you try to do a lot of exercise without warming up. The result is a day or two of sore muscles before you can move easily again. Your brain works in the same way. Your memory functions better when you feed it information in smaller doses over several days than if you stuff it full all at once. You will feel a lot more comfortable with your speech if you live with it for a few days.

Step 2: Decide what you are going to talk about.

You are probably saying, Hey, wait a minute! My teacher just told us we have to talk about the Constitution for our speeches. It's already decided.

True, your teacher may assign the subject you have to talk about. But *you* get to decide what part of that subject will make a good talk. So how do you decide that?

Think about your audience.

No problem, you say. You've been told you have to give a speech in front of the class. But is the class the other students, your teacher, or both? Chances are, the thought of speaking in front of the school nurse would make you nervous, let alone before all your classmates *and* your teacher sitting there with a red marker and a grade book.

Your first audience is YOU! If you were sitting in your chair, listening to someone talk about the Constitution, how long do you think you could keep your eyes open if you heard a speaker talking about a bunch of dates and not much else? How many times would you yawn if someone tried to squeeze the whole story of the signing of the Constitution into five minutes?

Wouldn't you be more likely to stay tuned if a speaker talked about some of the fights the delegates got into at the Constitutional Convention? Wouldn't it be news to you that the delegates thought their discussions should be so secret they nailed shut the windows of Independence Hall during one of the hottest summers ever? Wouldn't you like to picture Ben Franklin arriving every day in a sedan chair carried by four strong men? Or have someone actually pretend to be one of the delegates?

These interesting angles about the Constitution are just the right size for a short speech. And if you please kids like yourself with a lively presentation of unusual facts, along with a few lively comments of your own, you're bound to please your teacher, too.

Get personal.

Get personal about the Constitution? Or about the life cycle of a moth? Or about a book you've read? How can you get personal about the usual subjects you have to discuss in a speech?

Use some of the thinking time you've budgeted for yourself to see if you can come up with some different ways of looking at your subject. For example, you might ask yourself what your life would be like without the Constitution. A little detective work in some children's books about the Constitution would show you that before there was a Constitution, each of the thirteen states had its own money. Can you imagine what it would be like to go from your home state to another state and have to change money at the border? If each state had its own military the way they did before the Constitution, you might see Ohio fighting a war with Pennsylvania! Or highways that stopped dead at each state's borders. And we wouldn't call ourselves the United States, either. Without our Constitution, each state would be like a separate country!

If you've visited Washington, D.C., you may

have seen the original Constitution in the National Archives building. A description of your trip would make a terrific speech, as would a "You Are There" description of Independence Hall in Philadelphia, if you've ever visited that city. Even if you haven't, you could read a few guidebooks and give a travel talk about this historic site.

Now suppose your subject has to be about the life cycle of a moth. How personal can you get about *that?* Well, you could talk about what might happen if a female moth laid her eggs in a box of Cheerios in your kitchen cabinet, something that can actually happen if you don't seal up cereal boxes or flour canisters. In your speech, you could point out that the moth eggs are so small, an unsuspecting person might eat them for breakfast without ever knowing it! Then you could describe the rest of the life cycle by describing how long it would take for the eggs to turn into caterpillars inside a cozy box of cereal before anyone would notice. A talk like this would help the kids in your audience connect to your subject in a funny way, yet the speech includes all the scientific information your teacher would expect.

If it seems too farfetched to imagine such a situation, you could simply give the facts about the life cycle of a moth but ask the class to imagine the events happening in a tree right outside your classroom.

No matter what subject you have to talk about, see if there is some way you can tie in your own experiences to it. If you can't think of any way to get personal about your subject, then try to look at the human side of it. True, you weren't even alive when the Constitution was signed, but you could research information about someone who was there and pretend to be that person.

Maybe there's no way to get personal about certain subjects. If that happens to you, see if you can find some unusual or oddball facts about your topic. Many listeners enjoy learning trivia about familiar subjects.

Think small.

You may be wondering how on earth you are going to fill up three or five whole minutes or so with your speech. What are you going to say that will last that long? Or maybe you have the opposite problem and worry about how to cram your great-big subject into just five minutes.

The trick is not to talk about your *whole* subject but about one interesting part of it. Believe it or not, you will find more to talk about if you focus your subject a bit. Think about this comparison between focusing a photograph and focusing a speech subject.

If you were visiting the Grand Canyon, like many tourists you would probably want to take a few pictures of the whole thing, with someone standing in front of it. Is it possible to get the whole Grand Canyon into a 3″ × 5″ photo? The truth is that any photographer who tried to capture all that would probably wind up with a small dot standing in the middle of a big, orange blur. A better way would be to take a close-up shot of some part of the Canyon — say a prickly cactus against some red rock. Or a lizard sunning itself on the colorful rock face. Or maybe just a rock casting an interesting purple shadow. These are possible ways to focus a picture.

To focus in on the kinds of big subjects you get in a speech assignment, think about one part of the subject instead of the whole thing. The smaller and more specific you make your subject ahead of time, the easier it will be to prepare your speech.

Step 3: Take notes on your subject.

Now maybe you're sitting there thinking hard about ways to get other kids interested in your subject. And you've thought a lot about how to tie in your subject to your own experiences. On top of that, you know you have to keep your subject down to a size you can manage in just a few minutes. Still, you can't quite picture how you're ever going to get a hold of subjects like, say, the state of Texas, or photosynthesis, or even your scariest experience. Where are you going to find some odd but interesting information about your big, boring subject?

You can already feel your eyes glaze over as you picture yourself having to read column after column of dull facts from the encyclopedia. And you get a headache just thinking about trying to use the *Magazine Index* machine at your library without electrocuting yourself! Do you really have to go digging around just to get enough information to fill up five minutes or so of dead air? It depends.

Preparing a speech about yourself.

If you're lucky enough to get a speech assignment that's supposed to be about your personal experiences — say, your favorite foods, books, or hobbies — the best encyclopedia is the one in your head. So instead of trudging off to the library, spend your research time thinking about what you are an expert in. Maybe you have a great baseball card or sticker collection. Or maybe you are the leading authority on seashells in your class.

No matter what kind of speech you are going to give, you will need to take notes on separate index cards (3″ × 5″ are the best) or sheets of notebook paper divided into squares. Okay, you're wondering, how come I can't just write everything out on a sheet of paper?

Actually, you can, particularly for speeches on

personal subjects in which you are going to be listing ideas and details rather than research facts. But if you choose to take notes on a sheet of paper, leave several lines between each detail, fact, or idea you list. Then be prepared to cut each entry apart so that you can group and move them around when you get to Steps 5, 6, and 7.

Note cards or small squares of notebook paper also encourage you to keep related ideas in separate groups. And later on, when you pull your speech together, your ideas will already be on note cards. Most professional speakers use note cards rather than sheets of paper because they can flip through each idea one by one without having to run down a long list. It's hard to locate ideas on a long sheet of paper and talk at the same time.

Now let's say you want to give a talk on your hobby — collecting and classifying seashells. You will want to get your best information together for your speech. Here's how to do it. On your cards you would write down names of shells you own and a few words about them — the type of shells they are, words that describe their shape and texture, where they are found, and so on. On other cards you would list reasons you like shelling, places where shells can be found, a phrase or two describing what you do with your collection, and reasons why other kids might enjoy shelling.

Here's what some sample note cards on this subject might look like:

BIVALVES (2 shells)	
angel wings	jingle shells
jackknife clam	scallops
Kitten's paw	oyster
dipper shell	

UNIVALVES (1 shell)
helmet shell
cone shell
cowries
conch

CAPE COD SHELLS

oyster

jackknife clam shells

SHELLS FROM GULF

conch

cowries

REASONS
gives you something to do at the beach
make presents (jewelry, frames, boxes, collage)
arrange them by colors, bivalves, univalves, where they came from
show shells from diff. places
bring in things I've made (jewelry + boxes)

When you have a pile of a dozen or so cards —
the more the better — you will be ready for Step
4.

Preparing a speech on an unfamiliar subject.

Personal speeches are fairly easy to research
because you are already the expert. However, if
your science teacher wants each student to talk
about one kind of undersea life, and you've never
even been to the ocean, you will have to *become* an
expert. That means a trip to the library to dig up
some information on the subject.

A terrific source for ideas and subjects are children's simple nonfiction picture books. Writers for
young children highlight the most exciting facts
and provide large illustrations as well. Books like
these can give you loads of ideas in a short amount
of time.

To track down some good books on your subject,
here's what to do when you get to the children's
section of the library. Go to the Subject Card section
of the card catalogue and look up any card about
your assigned subject; OCEAN, for example. (On
the following page you can see what one of these
cards looks like.)

16

```
OCEAN
J         A first look at seashells
594       Selsam, Millicent
S         A first look at seashells,
          by Millicent E. Selsam;
          illus. by Harriet Springer.
          Walker and Co. 1983
```

The number on the left, the call number, tells you where in the nonfiction section of the bookshelves you will find books about oceans. Since you are doing a simple speech, you really don't have to go through all the cards. Instead, go to shelves where books with that call number are located.

When you get there, browse through any books that look appealing. Check out one general book about oceans that looks easy to read. Then see if you can find one book that is just about one kind of ocean life; say, seashells, fish, sea mammals, or ocean plants.

Try to pick a large-sized book with beautiful and clear pictures in case you want to use it as a visual aid in your speech later on. (There's nothing like a visual aid to get kids watching and listening to what you have to say. And holding up a book for everyone to see gives you something to do with your shaky hands.)

As you skim the children's books from the library or check information in the easiest encyclopedia you can find, here is how you would prepare a set of note cards.

The Table of Contents or the Index might give you some good headings for your cards. For example, you could write a card for each of these chapter headings: What Are Seashells?, What Are Univalves?, Meet Some Bivalves, How to Start a Collection, Making Things With Seashells. Any *one* of these would make a good speech topic. After skimming the best book you have and listing some subjects, turn to the chapter that now seems the most interesting to you; let's say, Meet Some Bivalves.

The rest of your note cards should each list information about bivalves — what they are, how they are different from univalves, what they look like, examples of this type of shell.

Now, maybe in a million years you can't picture yourself giving a speech about seashells. Maybe you're thinking: What about baseball cards, bottle caps, stickers, softball — things you really know something about? Or maybe you're faced with talking about the Bill of Rights, or fruit flies, or raising money for your Scout troop — subjects you don't know too much about. No matter what your speech topic is, you will still need to take some kind of notes on cards or pieces of paper you can group and organize later on. If your subject is something you know plenty about already, get as much of that information as you can in writing. If you get an assigned topic you haven't got a clue about, check out some simple kids' books, take notes on an interesting part of the subject, and become an expert on that!

Using visual aids.

After you have written your note cards, ask yourself if there is some part of your subject that you can *show* to your listeners. Are there objects you can bring in, like seashells, baseball cards, stickers, or rocks that will really bring your subject to life? A picture or drawing of angel wing shells, or jackknife clams, or the real shells themselves will say a lot more about what bivalves are than a bunch of words.

Visual aids can be a big help in getting your listeners involved in your subject. On the other hand, they can also distract your listeners from your message if they don't tie in directly with what you are trying to say or if they are too small for the whole group to see. So make sure that any visual aids you plan to use will really help you get your speech across.

Maybe you have your own photographs, slides, drawings, posters, or even a video on your subject that you can show to the class — with your teacher's permission, of course. Or you may want to use the blackboard to get your subject across visually. If possible, see if you can put your information on the board before you give your speech, so that you can quickly point to it while you are speaking.

Whatever visual aids you use, make note of your plans on your cards so that you will remember when to use them. Keep in mind that you may have to make arrangements ahead of time to bring in equipment or use the blackboard. Find the pictures, clip the photographs, and mark the quotation or pages you might want to show or read from. Have all your materials ready before you get your speech in order.

Once you've completed your note cards or note sheets and gathered any materials you might want to use as visual aids in your speech, you've made a big dent in the speech assignment. Several of the hardest parts of preparing a speech are done.

Give yourself a break before you go on to Step 4. You deserve it!

2
Card Tricks:
Developing and Organizing
Note Cards

By the time you have completed the first few steps in preparing your speech, you will probably be within a couple of days of D-Day — the due date for actually delivering your speech. How on earth do you turn that small pile of cards or stack of notes into something you can talk about? What's next?

Step 4: Decide on the purpose of your speech.

The purpose of your speech, you may be thinking, is to keep from dying of embarrassment in front of the class! What other purpose could there be? To figure that out, think about your listeners again. If you were in the audience, would you want to learn new facts, be instructed in a new skill, see someone perform or make you laugh, listen to a story, or be persuaded to support a new idea?

Think about different kinds of speeches.

Before any speaker decides on the purpose of a speech, it's important to know what kinds of speeches there are. Here's a rundown of various kinds of speeches, each with different examples of talks on the same general subject of magic.

• *An informative speech* gives listeners facts and information about a subject. An informative speech about magic might have titles like these: "The History of Magic," "Famous Magicians," "Easy Magic Tricks Anyone Can Do," "A Magician's Secrets."

• *A how-to speech* demonstrates to the audience how to do something step-by-step. How-to speeches about magic might have these titles: "How to Become a Magician," "How to Perform Disappearing Coin Tricks," "A Beginner's Guide to Magic," "How to Put On a Magic Show," "How to Figure Out a Magician's Secrets."

• *An entertaining speech* uses humor and performance to keep an audience's attention. Of course, even if your subject is a serious one, you will always want to entertain your audience. But a speech that has entertainment as its main purpose focuses on the light side of a subject. For example: "Three Great Tricks to Impress Your Friends," "Jokes to Tell While Doing Magic," "What to Do if You Goof Up a Magic Trick." In each of these speeches, the speaker would actually perform the tricks or tell jokes during the speech.

• *A narrative speech* tells the audience a story about the subject. Many professional speakers feel the most comfortable with this kind of speech because it's a way to get personal with the audience. Even if someone has a different purpose in mind, a speaker will often begin a how-to or informative speech with a story. Telling a story in a speech or even just beginning a speech with a story is a great way to get the audience on your side. Narrative speeches about magic might go like this: "The First Magic Trick I Ever Did," "The Night I Forgot My Magic Hat," "Seeing David Copperfield in Person," "The Most Money I Ever Spent on a Magic Trick."

• *A persuasive speech* tries to convince or persuade listeners about an idea. Persuasive speeches about magic might have titles like these: "Magic: The Best Hobby There Is," "Bored? Take Up Magic," "Magic, a Great Way to Make Friends."

No matter what kind of speech you plan to give, first ask yourself: What do I want my listeners to feel, learn, know, or experience? When you can answer these questions, you're on your way to deciding on just the right purpose for your speech.

Add up your information.
All those note cards and lists you've written also

point to a special purpose for your speech. If most of the information you've gathered on the subject of magic is about a favorite trick you've done dozens of times, then you're right in thinking you ought to demonstrate the trick for your audience.

On the other hand, if most of your cards or lists are filled with different kinds of magic items, then the purpose of your speech might be to tell your audience what they would need to buy to get started as a magician.

If you can't get rid of the memory of a birthday party where your five-year-old cousin kept giving away your magician's secrets, then a storytelling speech would be a great bet.

Finding just the right angle for your speech takes a bit of practice. If you still can't figure out what the purpose of your speech ought to be, try this:

• See if you can come up with more information about your subject.

• Show your notes to a family member, class-mate, or your teacher and ask for some help in figuring out what the purpose of your speech should be.

Step 5: Organize your notes according to the purpose of your speech.

Lay out your note cards.

Now you need to take a good look at all the

information you've gathered. If you have lots of good stuff about famous magicians, then group those cards together and put them in order. You might want to talk about early magicians first, then move on to a discussion of magicians who came on the scene later. Or maybe in doing your research you came across a great quotation by a well-known magician who talks about famous magicians who influenced him. The card with the quotation would be on top, followed by cards about magicians in the past.

Take out unnecessary note cards.

All your cards should tie right into the purpose of your speech. Throw out the one that tells you about Houdini if what you plan to do is show how to make a coin disappear. Get rid of the card about the early days of magic if you plan to tell your classmates about what equipment they'll need to get started in magic.

Add new cards to complete your information.

By now your stack of cards or note sheets may be looking pretty skimpy, and you might have doubts about how you're going to get a three- or five-minute speech out of what you have. Don't worry. What's important right now is making sure that each card is about one angle of your big subject and nothing else. It's better to have four cards about one idea than twenty cards about four ideas.

So how do you make sure you have enough information for a speech?

• Add more details, not more ideas. If you plan to talk about one famous magician, go back to your books and find a few more interesting tidbits about him or her. Don't add any new magicians to the list; just do a bit more with what you have already.

• Find some lively quotations to tie into your speech.

• If it seems appropriate, think about including a visual aid in your talk if you haven't done so already.

Arrange the note cards in the order of your speech.
As you look over your note cards, keep in mind that effective speeches follow this pattern:

• *Introduction*: statement of the main idea of your speech
• *Body*: 3 or 4 supporting points that emphasize your main idea with examples, visual aids, statistics, and facts
• *Conclusion*: a wind-up that summarizes your main idea in some way

Are you wondering why most speeches sound different if they are supposed to follow this pattern? These three sections — introduction, body, conclusion — are the foundation of every speech. But what you, the speaker, build on that foundation makes your speech unique. Maybe you will decide to begin with a story or a joke. Perhaps you plan to back up your supporting points with a visual aid, other stories, or weird facts. You might end with a question to get your listeners wondering about what you've said. Or you might conclude by answering a question you asked at the beginning of your speech. Each speaker has a different way of using that three-part speech foundation.

The purpose of your speech is the most important guide you have to help you organize your notes. If your purpose is to teach a simple magic trick by demonstrating it, then you should organize your cards in this order: materials needed, first step, second step, third step, etc., wind-up.

For an entertaining performance of several of your best tricks, you would organize your cards in the order in which you plan to do your tricks and tell your jokes.

If you want to tell the story of how a five-year-old once messed up your magic routine, you would organize your cards in the order of the events that happened.

To persuade your audience that they ought to consider magic tricks as a great hobby, a grouping of the cards listing your reasons and arguments in order of importance would work best.

Depending on the purpose of your speech, you

can arrange your cards in chronological order, in order of the importance of the ideas you have, in cause/effect order, or problem/solution order. The great thing about having all your information on note cards is that you can move them around and see what arrangement works best.

Step 6: Recopy your note cards for the middle of your speech.

Once you have your ideas in order, you need to prepare the actual note cards you will use in your speech. Keep in mind that each note card should have just enough words on it to trigger your memory when you actually deliver the speech.

People who make a lot of speeches often recommend working on the middle of the speech first. Why? Well, first you have to know what you are going to talk about before you can introduce the information.

The middle of your speech is where you explain your subject and make it believable with facts, examples, personal stories, or details.

The middle of your speech is where you stay in touch with your listeners by making your subject interesting to them. You can do this by using visual aids — pictures, objects, charts, and so forth.

In the middle of your speech you can also tie in facts about your subject with your listeners' experience — "When Harry Houdini was our age, he . . ."

In the middle of your speech you can highlight your information by planning to use hand gestures or to raise or lower your voice to emphasize certain ideas.

In short, the middle of your speech is where you get to use all the neat information you found in your research or out of your own head — the odd facts, the weird stories, the surprising statistics, and so on.

How do you record all this stuff so that you'll remember it during your speech? On each card, write out in big letters one point that supports the main idea of your speech. Below that, list words, phrases, and examples that will help you remember your point and fix it in your listeners' minds. On the following pages is a sampling of note cards that will help you move along from point to point:

FIRST, YOU WILL NEED PROPS
TO GET STARTED
costume (cape or gypsy outfit)
wand
poster and stand (to announce
each trick)

NEXT, YOU NEED TO DEVELOP 3
OR 4 TRICKS
simple things kids have around (coins,
cards)
tricks you can do without a helper
tricks that involve audience

AFTER THAT, WORK ON "PATTER"
jokes
stories

AFTER THAT, PRACTICE A LOT
before a mirror
in front of family
video or audio tape

Notice how many of the cards begin with *connecting* words like these: "Let's start," "Now think about," "First, second, third," "Next," "Finally," "To sum up," or comparative words like: "the smallest, next in size, and finally, the largest." These connectors help you move smoothly from one point to the next and help your listeners move along smoothly, too. You will see that when you practice your speech, these connectors will serve as cue cards to trigger your memory of the information that follows.

As you prepare your final note cards for the middle of your speech, keep these helpful tips in mind:

• Stick to three or four supporting points, one to a card.

• Use connecting words and phrases to help you move easily from one point to the next.

• Number the cards in the order you plan to use them.

• Carefully choose just one or two of the best examples you have to back up those points.

• Have a plan for using visual aids so that you can work them into your speech smoothly.

• Write or print a little larger than you normally would so that you can read your notes easily.

• Skip lines between each new piece of information if you have room.

Step 7: Write out your opening and closing sentences.

Work on your introduction.

Once the middle of your speech is organized, you have a pretty good idea of what your subject is all about. That means you're all set to introduce it. Now it's time to plan carefully how you are going to get your listeners' attention and lead into your subject.

You could hire a trio of trumpet players to announce your turn to speak, but chances are you'll have to toot your own horn to get your speech underway all by yourself, and that takes a little preparation. What should you be shooting for in your introduction? At the start of your speech, you will want to:

• Create a good first impression.

• Grab your audience's attention.

• Give the listener the idea that what follows is going to be worth listening to.

• Make a connection between the audience and the subject you are going to talk about.

Whew! All that just for starters? Here's some good news to calm you down. Your introduction need only be a few sentences long. After all, the real meat of your speech — your facts, details, examples, statistics, stories, or visual aids — is in the middle, or body, of your speech, and that is already done. Even better, the material you have already organized will suggest just how to open your speech.

To clear the deck before you work on your opener, here are some yawn-producing introductions to *avoid*:

• Avoid saying you're there to talk.

• Avoid apologizing for mistakes you're worried about making. Always feel confident that even if you make mistakes — and you might not — you will be able to handle them.

• Avoid using an introduction that is cute all by itself but doesn't tie into the rest of your speech. Again, working on the middle of a speech first fixes the subject in your mind so that you will have a pretty good idea of how to launch your speech.

• Avoid saying: "Today I'm going to give a speech about . . ." While that may be true, this kind of very direct statement doesn't do much to get your listeners interested in what is going to follow. The terrific subject you have spent so much time on deserves a little more fanfare.

Okay, now that you know how *not* to start, what are some great openers?

• Start with a *question* or a few questions that you answer in the middle of your speech. Examples: "Did you know that magicians have been performing tricks for nearly two thousand years?" Or, "Do you know the difference between a moth and a butterfly?" Or, "Did you know that nearly one third of the passengers on the *Mayflower* were children, one of them a baby boy born enroute to the New World?" Questions like these get your listeners involved right off the bat because you give them a way to connect with your subject.

• Start with a *statistic*. Examples: "Butterflies get a lot of attention, but moths ought to get even more because there are eight to ten times more moths on our planet than butterflies!" Or, "Even if you live thousands of miles from the nearest ocean, you can still collect hundreds of the nearly eighty thousand kinds of shells that exist in the world, a lot of them waiting to be discovered on mountainsides, fields, swamps, and forests."

• Start with a *story* about your subject. Examples: "If Harry Houdini hadn't sneaked off to a circus when he was just eight years old, he might have become a rabbi, like his father, instead." Or, "Last summer when I was on vacation during a cloudy, boring week, I discovered there was more to the beach than just sand."

• Start off with a *startling opinion* or *statement*. Examples: "Elmwood Middle School is one of the few schools in the area that doesn't give its students any free periods!" Or, "If you think only little old Victorian ladies in high button shoes collect seashells, you're wrong!" Or, "Put some magic — and some money — into your life by creating magic shows for kids' birthday parties."

• Open with a *quotation*. Example: "The giant brontosaurus/Was a prehistoric chap/With four fat feet to stand on/And a very skimpy lap."

• Start with a *definition*. Example: "Photosynthesis probably sounds like something you need a camera for, but it's just the way plants use light to make food."

• Make a *comparison*. Example: "If schoolwork is supposed to be like the work our parents do, then why do we have to do homework on weekends?"

• Use an *example* from real life. Example: "On summer nights, kids everywhere like to trap fireflies and watch them glow, but very few people know how fireflies light up."

Your introduction and conclusion are the only parts of your speech that you will need to memorize. Therefore, write out your opening sentences completely on a single note card. And remember to write or print very clearly and leave a space between lines if you have room.

Write your conclusion.

After all this work, your speech deserves just the right ending. Even if you forget your lines, leave out an important fact, or get your tongue twisted halfway through the speech, you can still save the day with your conclusion. Since the ending is the last thing your listeners will hear, make it direct and make it clear. Here are some tips on what *not* to do:

• Avoid introducing any new material in your conclusion.

• No matter how badly you think you may have bungled your speech, don't apologize. Just try to have an ending on hand that you can read straight from your cards if your memory deserts you.

• Stay away from multiple endings.

• Try not to end abruptly. If you make a special effort to tie your ending in with your introduction and the middle of your speech, this won't be a problem.

To come up with an ending that really works for you, try to get the same feeling across at the end as you did at the beginning. If you started funny, end funny. If you were trying to teach something in your speech, repeat why the skill or idea is important.

Here are several ways to recap your speech:

• If you began with a question, refer to it or repeat it with a twist and give the answer. Examples: "So why do you suppose magic has been around for two thousand years? Maybe it's because people want to believe in strange happenings and take part in something unbelievable." Or, "What happened to all those children, nearly a third of the *Mayflower* passengers, who came to the New World?

Many of their descendants are part of today's amazing American family."

• If you began with a statistic, repeat why it is important or how your ideas tie into it. Example: "Because there are so many more moths than butterflies, a collector can find interesting specimens almost anytime and anywhere, regardless of the season." Or, "Most people think you have to live near the ocean to collect shells, but there are thousands of inland shells to be found in swamps, forests, and meadows."

• If you told a story in your speech, tell your listeners how the events worked out for the characters or for you. Example: "So even though my magic show was practically ruined when my five-year-old cousin revealed all my secrets, I still had one more trick up my sleeve."

• If you used a quotation, make mention of it again in your wind-up. Example: "Although the rhyme said the brontosaurus was prehistoric, scientists still study it today."

• If you began your speech with a definition, recap it at the end. Example: "Now that you know photosynthesis doesn't have anything to do with cameras but is really a way that plants use light to make food, you can better understand why leaves change colors in the fall when daylight gets short."

• If you made a comparison to raise an argument in your introduction, use it again to remind your listeners of why your views are valid. Example: "Weekend homework should be abolished. After all, grown-ups keep telling us schoolwork is like their work, but they don't usually have to work on weekends. Kids shouldn't have to, either!"

• Mention an example from the beginning of your speech at the end to tie your ideas together. Example: "So the next time you catch fireflies in a jar, you will know that they get that special glow from a chemical that's triggered when fireflies of the opposite sex are around."

• You can also wind up your speech by summarizing your main points. Example: "If you want a great hobby you will never outgrow, consider learning magic. It's a great way to make friends, keep yourself busy, and even make money once you become good at it."

• Involve your audience by asking them to take action on some of the things you've said in your speech. Example: "Let your Student Council homeroom representative know how you feel about the subject of homework on weekends. If everyone sticks together on this issue, maybe we can change this policy in our school."

With endings like these, you really can leave your listeners with a clear idea of what you said. That's why it's worth writing out your last sentence or two and learning it by heart the way you did your introduction.

3
Speakeasy:
Practicing and Delivering
Your Speech

Here's the easy part. A couple of nights before your speech, go to your closet. Look through your clothes. Find that lucky sweater or favorite shirt that always makes you feel great. Dig out that soft pair of pants or the skirt with the comfy pockets. You know — the ones you wear when you're going out to eat or to a movie. Make sure your favorite things are clean and ready to wear the day of your speech. Looking good and feeling comfortable in your favorite or "lucky" clothes will give you an extra boost of confidence on the day of your speech.

Step 8: Try out your speech and make any needed changes.

Now that you know what you're going to wear, it's time to practice what you're going to say. Gather your cards, your visual aids if you have any, and find a private spot in your house where there's a mirror. If you have a tape recorder, bring that along, too, and make sure there's a watch or clock in the room so that you can time your speech. For now, keep away any pesky family members who might make you feel self-conscious. After all, this is just a rehearsal, so you don't need an audience yet.

Read over your cards.

Read your cards aloud several times to get a feeling of the words and the way your ideas connect. Each time you read, try to lengthen the amount of time you look up from your notes.

Memorize your introduction.

Recite your opening lines several times until you can say them without reading each and every word. If you have a tape recorder, record your introduction and keep playing it back until you can "hear" and "picture" the words in your mind.

Add new information to the introduction.

Recite your introduction again, but this time add on the next piece of information from your note cards. Practice this combination a few times. When that sounds pretty smooth, add a new piece of information to what you have practiced so far. As you practice, go through this process. Each time, begin with the introduction and add a new section. Then go back to the beginning, recite what you have learned so far, then add another new section. Do this until you have added each new section from your note cards to the whole speech.

Keep in mind that all you will really need to memorize is your introduction and your conclusion. What you are memorizing in the middle section of your speech is the *order* of your ideas, not the words themselves.

Memorize your ending.

Once you have run through your introduction and the middle, or body, of your speech and can recite it fairly well without reading too much of it, spend a few minutes learning your ending by heart. Do this by reading the ending several times and recording it if possible. Then try to deliver it without looking at the words on your cards.

Recite and time your speech.

Once you can get through your speech fairly well, recite it again and see how long your delivery takes. If your speech goes over the assigned time limit, cross out a few details from your cards and time your speech again.

If you end too soon, try speaking a bit more slowly. Many new speakers tend to rush their speeches to get them over with as fast as possible.

But since you have worked so hard to create an interesting speech, give yourself plenty of time to share all of that terrific information with your listeners.

Step 9: Practice the final version of your speech.

Practice before a mirror.

Once you have tightened up your speech, or expanded it a bit, it's time to deliver it in front of your favorite audience — you!

Walk up to the mirror, head held high, give yourself a big smile, set your cards and visual aids before you, and plunge right into your introduction. You probably know most of it by heart at this point, so you can look yourself in the eye and deliver it without having to read each word.

After your introduction, flip the first card under the rest of the pack. Look for the cue word on your next card — the first word in big letters. That should trigger your memory of the rest of the information on the card.

If you forget a word or a line, keep going, just as if you were in front of an audience. Keep in mind that actors who flub lines, like gymnasts who stumble in front of an audience, don't stop performing or start over — they move on and hope that the audience won't notice what they missed. After all, none of your listeners has read your speech. If you miss a line and keep going, they won't have any idea of what's missing.

Practice in front of someone.
If possible, give yourself enough practice time to deliver your speech in front of a friend or family member. If you can get a few people together, even better. Seat your listeners across the room from yourself so that you can get used to projecting your voice farther than usual. Smile before you begin. Look around the group. Then make eye contact with one person and begin your introduction. As you begin each new point on a card, make eye contact with another person. Slide each card under the bottom of the pile as you complete it. Work your visual aids into your speech wherever you indicated to do so on your cards.

Even if you forget a line, don't start over. Just move on to your next point as if that were the next line in your speech. If you want to emphasize something, use your hands to make the point. Smile in the places where that feels comfortable.

If you can't get anyone to listen to your speech and you have a tape recorder, tape the final version of your speech to see how it sounds. Put the tape recorder across the room so that you can see if you are speaking loudly enough to be heard from the back.

Take notes on anything you think could be improved when you give the live speech — things like *Slow down, Speak more clearly, Sound cheerful, Wait for the laugh after the joke*. Then play your tape back until you can hear it backward and forward.

Double check your visual aids if you plan to use any. Make sure you have clipped pages or pictures you want to show. Check that your equipment, if any, is in working order. Gather up the objects you plan to bring along.

Step 10: Deliver your speech.

Get yourself psyched.

The night before your speech, picture yourself going through the motions of your speech, from the time your teacher calls you up before the class until your closing words. Picture every detail —the way you will look in your favorite outfit, the way you will slowly walk to the front of the class or stage, the way you will smile at your audience and look around the room before you begin, the way you will make eye contact with a new person each time you move on to a new card, and the way you will say thank you and walk back to your seat with a big smile of success on your face.

Don't stay up all night sweating the awful things that might happen. Instead, think positive. Tell yourself you know you've prepared a great speech and that you're the number one expert on your subject.

Remember that one way political advisors help candidates relax before a big debate or speech is by having them spend the last few hours before the speech doing something other than practicing. If you have practiced for a couple of nights and have followed all the steps so far, you'll do a better job if you rest up instead of overrehearse.

Feel confident about your appearance.

Wear that favorite shirt or those comfy pants. Comb your hair or put it in a ponytail to keep it off your face. Check that you've brushed away the toast crumbs from your mouth so that you won't be worrying about them when you stand in front of your audience!

Make sure you pack everything you need for your speech — your note cards, your visual aids, or even the lucky coin you always carry in your pocket.

Your speech begins as soon as you walk into the room in which you are going to give your talk. Walk in a little taller than usual. Sit up in your seat with your head up, your shoulders a bit squared, and your hands clasped. There's no reason you should slink into the room or sink into your chair if you've done all your work. Getting into position right away sets you up for success the same way a runner, swimmer, or diver gets ready to move.

Control your nerves while you wait.

Unless you are the first speaker to go on, try to listen to the other speakers as if you weren't about to go on yourself. Get involved with what *they* are saying. If you are going to do anything besides listen attentively, just take long, slow, deep breaths to calm down those butterflies fluttering around inside you. Clench and unclench your fingers and toes if you can do so without looking weird. That's a great relaxing exercise.

Step up with confidence.

When your name is called, move out of your seat as smoothly as you can. Stand tall, walk confidently to the front of the class, and . . . smile before you ever say your first word. Remember, you've already done a great job, so you have a lot to smile about.

Line up your visual aids and cards in the order you plan to use them. Plan to hold your cards unless you are worried about shaky hands. You can always pick them up later.

If people are shifting around or are noisy, wait for everyone to settle down before you begin talking. Look over the whole room to draw everyone in, then find a friendly face in the crowd, make eye contact, and go straight into your introduction. If you draw a blank, simply read the introduction you wrote out. Seeing those familiar words again will get you right on track.

Use your voice to make your points.

With all that energy bubbling inside you, you may be tempted to race through all your terrific information. If you feel that happening, deliberately slow yourself down. You can do this by repeating or emphasizing important details. For example: "There are over eighty thousand kinds of sea-shells." (*Pause*.) "Eighty thousand!"

A pause at the end of each main point you make is another great way to give your listeners a chance to absorb the information and get ready for your next idea. A pause gives you time to relax, take a long, slow breath, and set up your next point. Speakers are sometimes afraid of dead air and try to fill it up with "uhs," "umms," and "you knows." A pause between ideas — even a long pause — gives a sense of importance to what you have just said or are about to say. Don't diminish that importance by clearing your throat or throwing in mumbled sounds. Pause instead.

Follow this same pattern for each point in your speech: Bring up a new card, make eye contact with another friendly face, then talk to that person. If you do this, you won't have any trouble finding that cheerful conversational tone of voice that all good speakers use.

If you lose the thread of what you were planning to say, just flip to the next card. Don't fiddle through your notes trying to track down that statistic or quotation. Just move on as if nothing happened and, chances are, no one will notice.

Use gestures to make your points.

If you feel yourself getting comfortable during your speech and find you can do without your cards, by all means use your hands to emphasize a good point in your speech.

If you are appealing to your listeners to be on your side, extend your hands toward them to drive home the idea that you are together on these ideas.

Use visual aids to make your points.

Visual aids are a terrific way to get that nervous-making attention off you and onto your message instead. Hold up your aids so that everyone can see what you are pointing to. This is a good time to ad lib, that is, throw in a few comments that may not be in your notes but may tie in to what you have said so far.

Wrap up your speech with confidence.

Save your longest pause for just before you deliver your conclusion. As you pause, look around at all your listeners. This will set them up for the closing of your speech and really give the feeling that you have made contact with all of them. Then read or recite your conclusion, making sure to look up after you say the last words, "Thank you."

No matter how well or poorly you think your speech has gone, keep you head high and walk slowly back to your seat. That's the last impression your listeners will have, and even if you forgot to tell them all about how the fireflies' lighting chemical works, act as if you did, and everyone will think you did.

Now that you know a little about how to work on a speech step by step, take a look at the next few chapters. There you will find out how to put together three very different kinds of speeches — a personal speech about a hobby, a history speech on a president, and a campaign speech for student government. Though each topic is quite different, you will see that the steps involved are all the same.

4
Speaking of You:
An Informative Speech

Imagine yourself in this situation. School has been underway for quite a few months. You've gone through stacks of notebook paper, dozens of pencils, and countless erasers. You've had homework almost every night and taken tests on everything from spelling to one-celled creatures. If you put all the compositions together that you have written this year, you would probably have a novel. And that doesn't even count the book reports, research papers, and the papier-mâché model of the planets you did for science. At the rate you're going, you could be ready for college by next year!

You may be wondering when your teacher is going to give everyone a break and let the class coast for a while. But nooo! Instead, you have just learned that the dreaded of dreaded assignments is due next week: A FIVE-MINUTE SPEECH! To soften the blow, your teacher announces that you can talk about yourself — maybe about your hobbies, an experience you had, your family, or a sport you enjoy.

There are groans all around the room. Sure, you and your classmates know how to speak up — sometimes when you're not even supposed to! But a speech??? With everyone watching you? How are you going to get out of this assignment without quitting school by next week?

Step 1: Make up a schedule to prepare your speech.

This part is easy. First take out your homework pad and a pencil. Write down "SPEECH DUE!!!" in huge letters on the due date. Then, in every space from now until that date, write down SPEECH again. Budget a couple of days for thinking about your subject and writing notes on it, and two or three days for practicing your speech.

Step 2: Decide what you are going to talk about.

Your teacher has already decided you are supposed to talk about yourself. But what part of you can you talk about without putting everybody to sleep?

When you get home and you read over the assignment, start thinking. What are a few things you know about that might be interesting to the kids — and your teacher — who are going to listen to you? What do *you* know about that they don't?

There's your collection of birds' nests gathering dust on a shelf in your room. But the more you think about it, the less interesting that seems. You only have three of them, and you don't even know what kinds of birds made the nests.

As you look around your room, you see lots of stuff you used to collect — bottle caps, souvenirs, seed pods — but all of it looks a little dusty and a little too young for the kid you are now.

Then you remember the big suitcase under your bed. It's full of magic tricks you've gotten as presents or bought with your allowance. Great stuff like stage makeup you got on sale after Halloween; the flyers you made up on your computer with your stage name, The Great Magifico; your black cardboard top hat; and, of course, your black cape.

As you sort through your stuff — the tablecloth, trick glass, prearranged deck of cards, the ropes, some of it homemade and some bought with your allowance — you realize you have a great subject to give a speech about: magic!

Step 3: Take notes on your subject.

You can hardly stop scrambling through all the great magic props you have to do something as boring as writing down ideas about magic. You have a million ideas, and pretty soon you have a bunch of note cards listing those ideas:

HOUDINI

might have become rabbi, not magician
thought rabbits were surefire trick
said to try old tricks new way

MAGIC SHOW
costumes
signs
jokes
assistant
start big, end big, reg. tricks
in the middle

HOW TO PRACTICE

practice "patter"

mirror or with somebody

try out diff. things

videotape or audio tape to
    hear how it looks/sounds

BEST TIPS

materials ready

practice, practice, practice

don't tell secret of a trick

keep going even with mistake — joke
    or laugh about it

end special way; don't trail off or say
    what's next / don't repeat tricks

DO DISAPPEARING DIME TRICK
visual aids: cape, hat, posters, dime,
envelope (already cut)
MONEY GROWS ON TREES TRICK
visual aids: oranges,
knife (glue on it), nickel

You're running out of note cards, you have so many ideas listed. You will have no trouble giving a five-minute speech; you have enough information to talk about magic for an hour! How are you going to decide what part of magic to talk about?

Step 4: Decide on the purpose of your speech.

As you look over your materials and spread out your notes, you realize you have enough information for four or five different speeches. Which one are you going to do? You consider showing kids how to put on a magic show, but then you realize you only learned how to do that after learning a dozen or so tricks. You wrote "Harry

Houdini" on one card because you got interested in magic after seeing a movie about him. That would be a great subject for a speech . . . until you realize you'd have to go to the library to get more information.

As you study all the notes you wrote down, you realize that a lot of the cards have to do with the basic rules and secrets of magicians. You remember that you didn't get successful in magic until you realized that the *way* a magician does a trick is more important than the trick itself.

You figure out that sharing a few simple magicians' tips might get kids interested in your hobby more than anything else.

Step 5: Organize your notes according to the purpose of your speech.

As you go through your cards, take out the ones about special props or unusual tricks — anything that doesn't tie in with your purpose. Then number the remaining cards in order of the most important tips a magician follows while doing a trick from start to finish.

In looking over the cards, you may notice that while you have a lot of advice to offer a beginner, something is missing — you and your magic. That's when you go back to the discarded card marked "Disappearing Dime Trick" and add it to the pile.

You decide that the best way to get the tips across is to use them to demonstrate this simple magic trick.

Step 6: Recopy your note cards for the middle of your speech.

If your cards look pretty neat, then move on to Step 7. However, if they are too confusing or messy, write out a heading for each group of ideas that go together. If you plan to use visual aids, make note of when you will do so.

Step 7: Write out your opening and closing sentences.

Remember, a speaker's job in the introduction is to make a good impression and give the listeners an idea of what is going to follow. A speaker should also try to get the audience on his or her side right away and get them involved.

The conclusion should give listeners a sense that the speaker has tied together the main idea presented in the introduction and developed in the middle. To give listeners a sense that the speech was clear (even if it wasn't) and that the speaker did what he or she set out to do (even if he or she didn't), try to echo the beginning of the speech at the end.

Here are several kinds of openers paired with endings that circle back to the beginning:

Question

Introduction: "Do you know that all good magicians share the same secret of success? (*Pause.*) Blackstone, Houdini, the great Thurston — all of them knew that the way a magician performs a trick is more important than the trick itself!"

Conclusion: "Now that you know the same secrets that made Blackstone, Houdini, and Thurston successful magicians, and you've seen how to use those tips to perform a simple trick like the one I did, you are ready to work your own magic. Before you try any trick, just tell yourself that the way you perform a trick is much more important than the trick itself."

Statistic

Introduction: "If nine out of ten magicians get lots of applause after their acts and the tenth one doesn't, it usually means the performer forgot a magician's greatest secret: The way a magician performs a trick is a lot more important than the trick itself."

Conclusion: "As you can see from the simple trick I did, I remembered how important it is to perform the trick with a little style. I'd rather do one simple trick well than ten flashy tricks badly."

Story

Introduction: "When I first began performing magic tricks, it seemed as if people just yawned or walked away. I didn't really get much reaction until I learned the most important secret that all good magicians know: The way you perform a trick is more important than the trick itself."

Conclusion: "I've been performing tricks for a couple of years now, and I usually stick with the simple ones I know I won't mess up. What I work on is my patter and my gestures to give even the simplest tricks more style."

Comparison

Introduction: "Performing a successful magic trick is like giving a good acting performance onstage. An actor can say all the lines but sound dull if he doesn't have much expression. Magicians also need some style in performing tricks, and that's a magician's greatest secret."

Conclusion: "My favorite actors on TV and in the movies have funny ways of doing things. All the magicians I like also have their own style of performing the same magic trick, and that's what makes each magician special."

Step 8: Try out your speech and make any needed changes.

By the time a speaker reaches this step, he or she has a pretty good sense of the direction of the speech. And it's the direction or order of the speech that a speaker needs to memorize.

With all your cards and visual aids in hand, read your speech four or five times out loud in a quiet room a couple of nights before the due date. Tape recording the speech will help you hear any dead or confusing spots so that you can smooth them out.

At this stage, a speaker should learn the opening and closing lines by heart. Then it's time to try out the speech again and time it, adding or deleting details to come in close to the time limit.

Step 9: Practice the final version of your speech.

It's time to face your friendliest audience — you! Before a mirror, recite the speech you have practiced. Smile first, look yourself in the eye, then recite your introduction. Each time you flip a card, look up at yourself. Be sure to pause between each card, particularly before the end. Don't forget to say "Thank you."

If possible, try out your speech before someone sitting across the room from you. Or if you have a tape recorder, place it in the far corner of the room, recite your speech, and hear how it sounds when you play it back.

The night before, picture yourself going through each part of your speech, from walking up to the front of the class, smiling, then speaking, to finally saying, "Thank you" and walking with your head high back to your seat.

Step 10: Deliver your speech.

Your speech begins when you wake up on the day it's due. Make sure you're wearing a favorite comfortable outfit and that you look neat. Try to get to class a bit early if possible. Do a few deep breathing exercises while you wait your turn. Listen attentively to the speakers preceding you. Get involved with what they are saying so that you don't get overinvolved in your nervousness.

When you get up front, wait for everyone to settle down. As they do so, get your visual aids lined up in order, hold your cards firmly, and give everyone a big smile as you look around the room. Make eye contact with one person, then begin your introduction.

Sample speech
Based on the preceding steps, here is what a how-to speech about magic tips might sound like:

"Do you know that all good magicians share the same secret of success? (*Pause.*) Blackstone, Houdini, the great Thurston — all of them knew that the way a magician performs a trick is more important than the trick itself. (*Pause.*)

"A simple trick performed with these tips in mind will impress an audience a lot more than a flashy trick that the magician bungles. So before you go out and invest in a top hat and cape like the ones I'm wearing, learn these important tips: (*Pause.*)

"Have your materials ready.

"Practice each trick until you can do it smoothly.

"Practice what you are going to say with each trick.

"Practice in front of a mirror.

"Never, ever tell how you performed a trick.

"Don't tell the audience what is going to happen next. That way you can surprise them.

"Don't repeat tricks to the same audience.

"If you make a mistake, have a joke ready and keep going.

"End your trick in style — tip your hat if you have one, bow deeply, wave your cape if you are wearing one, toot a horn you have on hand, or simply sing: 'Ta-dah!' (*Pause.*)

"To demonstrate just how important these tips are, I will follow all of this good advice while performing a very simple trick. I have performed this trick before but not in front of any of you. I have practiced it in front of the mirror. And I now have my materials ready — this dime and this envelope. (*Pause.*)

"You see here this plain white envelope. May I have a volunteer to examine the envelope? (*Hold envelope in one corner while someone looks inside.*) May I have a volunteer to examine this dime? (*Have someone look at an ordinary dime.*)

"A plain envelope and a plain dime, Ladies and Gentlemen. May I have a third volunteer to put the coin in the envelope? (*Have someone put the coin in the envelope. Shake the envelope for all to hear, then let the dime slip into your hand through the pre-made slit in the corner of the envelope.*)

"Can you hear the dime inside the envelope? (*Wait for answer.*) Louder? (*Wait for response.*)

"Ladies and gentlemen, the dime has disappeared! (*Tear up the envelope in small pieces and throw them into the audience like confetti while concealing the dime between the ring and pinky finger.*)

"Will someone ask me to show how the dime disappeared? (*Wait for someone to ask.*)

"Never! Remember, one of the greatest magician's secrets is never, ever reveal how a trick was performed. With that I leave you, Ladies and Gentlemen! (*Deep bow. Then remove hat and cape.*)

"Now that you know the same secrets that made Blackstone, Houdini, and Thurston successful magicians, and you've seen how to use those tips while performing a simple trick like the one I did, you are ready to work your own magic. Before you try any trick, just tell yourself that the way you perform a trick is much more important than the trick itself.

"Thank you."

5
Speaking of Social Studies:
A Narrative Speech

Some people have all the rotten luck. This year, your class is studying American history, and each student has to give a speech about a former president. Do you get one of the interesting ones like George Washington, Thomas Jefferson, or Abraham Lincoln? Nooo. You get John Quincy Adams, not even the famous John Adams, but the *son* of the famous Adams.

Right away, you know you aren't going to get information about this speech out of your head. Even your social studies textbook has only a few sentences on him, and he doesn't even rate a picture. What are you going to do besides make plans to leave the country and go to a place that doesn't have presidents?

Step 1: Make up a schedule to prepare your speech.

Chances are you have a couple of weeks to get this kind of speech ready because it involves researching information in the library. Right away, set aside at least four or five days to get materials, read them, and take notes.

To give yourself a quick boost, go to the children's section of your school or local library *immediately* — the day you get the assignment or the next day at the latest. A fast start will give you first crack on the general books about presidents that all the other kids in your class will want, too. And getting your books early on will prevent you from catching a dangerous disease most students (and grown-ups) get when they have to do a big project, namely, PROCRASTINATIONITIS!

Step 2: Decide what you are going to talk about.

You are probably all too aware that your subject is John Quincy Adams. But look on the bright side. You could have gotten Chester Arthur or Millard Fillmore! At least Adams came from a well-known family.

Instead of wishing you could somehow change your subject to Franklin D. Roosevelt without anyone noticing, tell yourself you are going to find something interesting about John Quincy Adams, no matter what. Convince yourself there must be something the man did that kids your age will find interesting, funny, or unusual.

With that in mind, skim the general presidents' books you got from the library to learn the basic facts about John Quincy Adams's life. While you're doing that, you will probably find out that he was the only president ever who was the son of a president, an unusual fact, but not exactly something that will get kids rolling in the aisles. But keep it in mind. Maybe you can tie it into something else.

As you read through general information about Adams in various books about presidents, you learn that when he was a teenager, he was already working for the government in France. Hmm. That's a possible angle. Maybe you could compare what his teenage life was like to a teenager's life nowadays.

After you read the presidential fact books, quickly read through any books specifically about John Quincy Adams. You will probably find out that most paintings of him show a rather severe-looking man. This confirms what you are beginning to figure out — that growing up the son of a president and going to work at such an early age made John Quincy Adams very smart but not very happy.

Like his father, John rose at 4:30 A.M. every day

and always worked much harder than anyone else. He frowned upon most kinds of relaxation, and his idea of spending what little free time he had was taking long walks in the cold in Washington, D.C., which was fairly rural during his presidency. Swimming in the freezing waters of the Potomac River before dawn was another pursuit he allowed himself.

Then, in your research, you come across this nugget of information. One day during a challenge with his servant and his son, Adams wanted to prove that at the age of fifty-nine he could swim across the Potomac River as he once did as a younger man. Finding himself slowed down by his heavy clothes, he took everything off, swam the river, and landed nude on the shore while his valet went back to the White House to fetch him some dry things. For the first time, you start to see the man as a human being, not just the tireless speaker who turned listeners away with his endless arguments for his ideas.

That's when you decide to use the Potomac swimming story to show the kind of determined but very real person John Quincy Adams was.

Step 3: Take notes on your subject.

You know the swimming story is something that will help kids picture John Quincy Adams as more than a severe-looking statesman and politician. But since you're doing this speech as a class assignment, you are going to need to include more information than just that story. So take notes on Adams's important achievements so that you can show both sides of his personality.

Some of the notes might include this information:

CHILDHOOD / GROWING UP
only president who was son of a president
father + son spent time but no close feelings
very strict childhood
teenage years worked in govt. for father
traveled alone in Europe very young
wrote long political articles before 20
no chance to be normal kid

ACHIEVEMENTS/DISAPPOINTMENTS (1)
diplomat under father (Russia, Belgium, England)
helped with Monroe Doctrine
helped end War 1812 England
got Florida from Spain
president - not popular, couldn't get ideas
passed after his presidency

ACHIEVEMENTS/DISAPPOINTMENTS (2)
stubborn, impatient, not popular with people
not reelected, but not too proud to be in Congress fighting for same ideas
died in House of Rep. — 80 yrs. old

PERSONAL

up at 4:30 A.M.; long walks in cold;
swimming Potomac (story about
    swimming age 59, no clothes!)
same relationship with children as with
    father — never cared what
    people thought
stubborn husband/father

MISC. FACTS

Washington, D.C. still rural — cows
    at White House
no Secret Service; president could
    walk anywhere
JQA only president to be son of president ever
age 14, traveled from Russia to Holland; father
    didn't know where JQA was for 6 months!

Consider using visual aids, perhaps one or two pictures of John Quincy Adams looking like the serious and distinguished statesman he was — not the sort of person who would be swimming around in the Potomac River without clothes.

Step 4: Decide on the purpose of your speech.

By getting so much information in the first few steps, you realize that the purpose of your speech is to make John Quincy Adams more human by telling a story about his determination both as a politician and as a private person.

Step 5: Organize your notes according to the purpose of your speech.

The best part of your speech is going to be the swimming story. But for everyone to appreciate the story, you have to present the serious and dignified John Quincy Adams first so that your story makes a solid point.

Since your notes are already in chronological order, move on to Step 6.

Step 6: Recopy your note cards for the middle of your speech.

Throw out any cards that don't fit in with your

purpose. Stick to the main events of Adams's life since the focus is a personal story rather than a historical event. Audiences tend to nod off when a speaker throws out too many facts. Make sure your headings are clearly written so that you can look at them quickly and know right away what comes next.

Step 7: Write out your opening and closing sentences.

The heart of your talk is the story you plan to tell. To set it up so that it makes a point about John Quincy Adams's character, you will have to present the historical facts first. This doesn't mean you have to be dull. Here are several pairs of openings and conclusions that a speaker might use to frame the Potomac swimming story:

Visual Aid

Introduction: "I've brought in a couple of pictures to show you what the sixth President of the United States looked like during his lifetime from 1767 to 1848. (*Show picture.*) These pictures are important because they show the kind of person John Quincy Adams was, someone who never had a chance to be a kid or a teenager and who spent most of his life working on government business like . . ." (*List impressive achievements at different ages.*)

Conclusion: "This story about John Quincy Adams shows you how determined a man he was even when he was doing something for relaxation. Seeing him take on a personal challenge just for sport shows the incredible determination he had in every part of his life and explains why he was able to accomplish so much."

Question

Introduction: "Do you get John Adams and John Quincy Adams confused? I sure did. Both father and son spent most of their lives in politics, hardly stopping to be kids or teenagers before they took on the responsibilities of government like . . . (*List of achievements*.) Yet one experience that happened to the son, John Quincy Adams, which never happened to his father, was . . ." (*Begin story*.)

Conclusion: "The Adams family became famous for their achievements in government for several generations, and many people get them mixed up. But if you want to remember one thing that only John Quincy Adams did that no one else in his family did, picture him at the age of fifty-nine swimming across the freezing Potomac River, shedding his clothes to go faster, then making it to shore. That, too, shows another side of the great Adams family spirit!"

Startling opinion

Introduction: "I was hoping I would get George

Washington or Abraham Lincoln to talk about in my speech, not John Quincy Adams. But Adams did a lot of important things for our country, like helping to write the peace treaty that ended the War of 1812. And he was considered one of the greatest secretaries of state we ever had, working out important agreements with Spain and England. While he only served one, unsuccessful, term as president, he is regarded as one of the greatest diplomats in U. S. history."

Conclusion: "I already knew a lot about more popular presidents like Washington, Lincoln, and FDR. But now I'm glad I learned about someone who wasn't so popular, yet who was important to our country. Though John Quincy Adams couldn't get a lot of his plans through while he was president, many of them succeeded later, thanks to his stubborness and determination."

Step 8: Try out your speech and make any needed changes.

Telling a story well is like telling a joke well. You have to get across the events very smoothly and with details that help your listener *picture* what happened. In this speech, it is also important that you present your subject in a dignified way before you tell the story. So make sure you have enough interesting facts to show the historical side of John

Quincy Adams so that everyone can appreciate the human side in your story. He certainly accomplished much during his career, so you should be able to lead off with some important achievements.

Step 9: Practice the final version of your speech.

This is a good dinner table speech. Your family will probably be expecting to hear a lot of dry facts about a president, not a good story. Trying out your speech in a casual setting will help you get in a storytelling mood.

Step 10: Deliver your speech.

When your name is called, walk up to the front of your class. Line up your visual aids, if any. Take your note cards in hand, smile, look over the whole class, then make eye contact with one person and begin your introduction. Pause between your introduction and the beginning of your story. Direct your eye contact to another listener in the room and continue on. Save your longest pause between your story and your conclusion. Look at the whole group again, find one person to address, and recite your conclusion. Don't forget to say, "Thank you." Pause a moment, smile, then go proudly back to your seat.

Sample speech

Based on the preceding steps, here is what a narrative speech about John Quincy Adams might sound like based on the notes in Step 3:

"I was hoping I would get George Washington or Abraham Lincoln to talk about in my speech, not John Quincy Adams. But John Quincy Adams did a lot of important things for our country, like helping to write the peace treaty that ended the War of 1812. And he was also considered one of the greatest secretaries of state we ever had, working out important agreements with Spain and England. While he only served one term as president and didn't get much done during his term, he is regarded as one of the greatest diplomats in U.S. history. (*Pause.*)

"However, I just couldn't get much of a sense of what he was like as a private person. People remember George Washington's truthfulness when they think of the cherry tree story, and everyone can picture Abe Lincoln chopping wood. But it's hard to identify with John Quincy Adams because he didn't grow up like most kids.

"First of all, he was the son of a president, John Adams, the second President of the United States, and Abigail Adams, the second First Lady of the United States, so he grew up in the White House. Also, John Quincy Adams started doing government work for his father when he was just fourteen —

only four years older than we are right now! It's hard to picture someone like that being real.

"Then I came across a great story about John Quincy Adams that showed me what he was like when he wasn't being president, and it's a story I'd like to tell you about. (*Pause.*)

"Picture the White House in 1825 with cows grazing on the lawn, and picture Washington, D.C., as a place where even the President of the United States could walk around without getting too much attention. Imagine the spot near the Potomac River where the Lincoln Memorial now stands. Then picture John Quincy Adams (*point to a picture of him in a book*) and his manservant — there were no Secret Service men back then — rowing a small boat across the river from that spot so that Adams could swim back the one-mile width of the river.

"It was early morning, cold, dark, and windy, and John Quincy Adams was determined to do at age fifty-nine what he'd done as a younger man, swim across the Potomac River. He was just as stubborn and determined about this personal challenge as he was about political challenges — like getting new roads built, aiding education, exploring the country, and developing its natural resources. He never gave up fighting for those plans and did not give up his swimming plan, either, even when the rowboat capsized.

"Instead, John Quincy Adams plunged into the

chilly Potomac, took off his heavy clothes, and swam to the far shore, then all the way back, just as he had planned. Though he was exhausted and breathless, he ordered his servant to get him some dry clothes back at the White House. Then he rested on shore — without any clothes on — and waited for the servant to return with his things.

"John Quincy Adams did a lot more than swim across the chilly Potomac River when he was fifty-nine. He went on to show the same determination he had when he was a congressman in later years. In fact, he was a more successful congressman than president and wasn't too proud to run for this lesser office. He never gave up on his ideas no matter how unpopular they were. This kind of stubborness kept him fighting for his ideas until he was eighty years old, when he died while waiting to speak before the House of Representatives.

"I already knew a lot about more popular presidents like Washington, Lincoln, and FDR. But now I'm glad I learned about someone who wasn't as popular, yet who was important to our country. Though John Quincy Adams didn't get a lot of his plans through while he was president, many of them succeeded later on, thanks to his stubborness and determination.

"Thank you."

6
Speaking of Opinions:
A Persuasive Speech

Now that you know how to put together speeches for different school subjects, you probably feel more confident as a speaker. Maybe you even feel confident enough to run for the student council in your school! The steps you follow to prepare a campaign speech are the same as those you would use to prepare any other kind of school speech.

Let's say you decide you want to run for the student council in your middle school. You are going to need posters, you are going to need ideas, and you are going to have to give a speech! Your first step is to complete Step 1 and plan a schedule for working on your speech. Then you are ready for the next step.

Step 2: Decide what you are going to talk about.

Maybe you think your school needs a new gym. Or that homework should be abolished. You know you could get plenty of votes if you said you would try to have eight months of school instead of nine! But even if students in your school want all of these things, do you think you have any chance of making them happen? Probably not.

Spend a couple of days with a notepad and talk to kids you know pretty well at school. Ask them what bugs them about school and what they think a student council representative could do about it. Ask them what one thing they wish school did or didn't do for the students. You will get a lot of crazy answers, but write them down anyway. Get as many opinions as you can.

When you get home, add your own ideas to the "wish" list. You should have a pretty long list of ideas by now. Go through each one and cross out those that are too weird or impractical for you to do anything about. Then go through the remaining list and circle any ideas — yours and any others — that make sense and you think you can do something about.

Maybe the biggest issue on kids' minds has to do with time — not having enough free time during school or at home because school schedules are too tight and homework loads are too heavy.

Consider whether there are things you could do to improve this problem. Do you think so? Then you've got your campaign issue — finding ways to give students more free time in school. That's what you are going to try to work for if you get elected.

Step 3: Take notes on your subject.

The more you think about it, the more excited you get about running for student council. Maybe there are things you could do to give students more free time. List each of your ideas on a card. Then let people know that's what you are going to work for. Ask for other students' ideas and list those, too. If you have friends or relatives at other schools, find out how much free time students have in those places. You might want to surprise your opponents with some statistics no one else has. Consider calling a couple of schools in other towns and asking about the free periods there and the homework policy. Solid facts will help your campaign a lot more than vague promises. After you have all your statistics, your notes might include information like this:

RESEARCH OF STUDENT REASONS/COMPLAINTS (50+KIDS)
no homework
daily pizza
lounge
homework robot! (good joke for speech)

OTHER PLACES
good students get more time
more time between classes common
extend lunch hour 10 minutes
after-school program
one free period a week
free periods for B+ or better students

CHANGES I'LL MAKE
abolish study periods
shorten homeroom period and give time to kids
start school later
less homework — more free time
lengthen between-class time to 5 min.
everybody — 2 free periods/wk.
B+ students — free period every day

Step 4: Decide on the purpose of your speech.

Since you got yourself pretty well focused in Step 2, the purpose of your speech should be pretty clear. Your purpose is to *convince* students that as student council representative you will work to give them more free time in school.

Step 5: Organize your notes according to the purpose of your speech.

As you go through all your great ideas, decide which ones are the strongest, number those at the beginning of your pile, and throw out any cards that don't belong. Stick to three or four of your best ideas so that kids will know exactly what you stand for.

Step 6: Recopy your note cards for the middle of your speech.

As you look over your note cards, check that you have used strong *action* words so that your listeners will see you as a person who can get things done. Make sure you use words that are *specific*, not vague. "I will discuss getting students one free period a week at the very first meeting of the Student Council." That sentence is a lot more specific than saying: "I plan to talk to the Student Council about free time as soon as possible."

Step 7: Write out your opening and closing sentences.

Many politicians lose votes by sounding too nervous, too vague, or too weak when they begin a debate, speech, or press conference. You need to get across in the first sentence what you stand for.

Look over the ideas you have planned for the middle of your speech. What can you say about *all* of them that will get you off to a good start?

How can you wind up your speech so that everyone is very clear about why you are the best candidate? Here are some possible openers and conclusions:

Question/Statistic

Introduction: "Do you know how much time you spend in school? Thirty-six hours a week. Do you know how little of that is free time? Just two-and-a-half hours! I have a plan for changing those numbers, so that you have more time to see your friends or just relax between classes."

Conclusion: "Wouldn't you like to increase your free time at school from two-and-a-half hours to six hours a week? As I have demonstrated, I have a realistic plan for giving you more free time. Elect me to the Student Council, and you will have time on your hands — free time!"

Statistic

Introduction: "The biggest complaint most students have in this school isn't the cafeteria food but lack of free time. Nearly seven out of ten students I interviewed said overloaded schedules were the worst thing about going to school. I intend to do something about that."

Conclusion: "Since lack of free time is the number one problem the majority of students in our school complain about, that is the number one problem I am going to work on if you elect me to the Student Council."

Other introductions and conclusions might include these: You could tell a story about how you expected that most kids wanted a change in homework policy, but you found out that what they really wanted was more free time in school. You could compare how other middle schools give students more free time than yours. You could be daring and ask how many people in the audience would like more free school time.

Regardless of what kind of introduction you write, make sure you repeat it back with a twist at the end. This gives your listeners a clear idea of what you have said and what you will do. A clear finish can really leave a strong impression even if you muddled through the middle.

Step 8: Try out your speech and make any needed changes.

Find a quiet place at home to rehearse your speech. Remember to read the entire speech all the way through several times to get the flow of the words going. Then memorize your introduction and go back to it as you add each point. Finally, memorize the end.

As you listen to your speech on tape or in your head, make sure that each point is absolutely clear. Remember, this time you are talking about a subject everyone has opinions about. So it's even more important to make sure your main idea and supporting points tie in very clearly. Cross out anything that doesn't drive home your main opinion or distracts from it.

Emphasize your opinions with words like: "In the first place," "Second, third, fourth, etc." "Most of all," "Above all," "As a result," "In spite of this." Connecting words like these not only will guide your listeners from point to point, these words suggest that you have a definite step-by-step plan for getting things done.

Finally, practice your speech in front of a mirror. Since you're brave enough to run for office, you're bold enough to use your hands to emphasize the strongest opinions you have. Try pointing to stress your main point. Don't be afraid to reach out to the crowd with both hands as if you are bringing them toward you and your ideas.

Time your speech so that it clocks in close to the specified time allotment. Political audiences tend to appreciate short, direct speeches over longer, windier ones. Think of your speech as a short commercial for yourself. Don't go overtime unless you want people to tune you out. You are better off finishing early than running over. This shows you are in control of some very definite, easy-to-understand ideas.

Step 9: Practice the final version of your speech.

Because you will probably be speaking before a larger group than usual, give yourself more practice time for a political speech than for a class speech. Try to tape record your speech to see how it sounds. If your school has audiovisual equipment, see if the AV person in charge is willing to videotape your speech ahead of time. This is a great way to see how you look and sound.

If possible, try out your speech where you will be delivering it — in the auditorium, cafeteria, or library. Wherever it is, try to project to the farthest corner of that room. Remember, a bigger group will be making more noise, so practice this kind of speech more loudly than the usual classroom speech.

Step 10: Deliver your speech.

To give yourself more authority, dress up just a bit more than you normally would to give your political speech. This doesn't mean dressing totally different than usual but looking a little sharper and maybe a little older than your everyday self. After all, most kids don't run for office but do like to think of the person that they will vote for as being a better version of themselves. So try to look the part.

If you are sitting onstage or in front of the room with the other candidates, don't forget that you are already giving an impression of yourself before you even begin talking. Plant your feet on the floor, clasp your hands on your lap, and stay that way while others are speaking. Give the other speakers respect by watching and listening to them attentively. This shows you are a generous opponent.

When your name is called, walk to the podium confidently. Put your note cards down. Smile at the crowd as you wait for them to settle down. Find a friendly face a few rows back and direct your introduction to that person. After each section of your speech, pause to slow yourself down and catch your breath. Then smile again, find a face in another part of the crowd, and move forward with your next point. Save your biggest pause for last. Look around at the entire group as you pause to set up your conclusion. Find a face in the middle of the crowd (this gives the impression you are speaking to each and every person in the audience) and move forward with your strong conclusion.

Take advantage of the applause by standing and smiling at the audience instead of rushing off. After all, they are applauding you! Go back to your seat after the clapping has stopped. Resume your attentive and respectful appearance as the following speakers talk, so that you maintain the strong impression you have made already (or correct a poor impression you may have made by mistake). Remember, you are on view as a candidate the whole time you are up front or even in the audience. Look like a winning candidate and you'll boost your chances of actually being the winner!

Sample speech

Here's what a speech based on the previous steps would sound like:

"Do you know how much time you spend in school? Thirty-six hours a week. Do you know how little of that is free time? Just two-and-a-half hours. I have a plan for changing those numbers so that you have more time to see your friends or just relax between classes.

"If elected, I plan to tell the Student Council what I learned while I was campaigning for this position. A lot of you will remember that a few weeks ago I went around the school and talked to over fifty of you (*point to audience*) to find out what bugged you about school or what you wished the school would do for the students.

"Some of you wanted pizza every day. (*Wait for laugh.*)

"A few people said no homework.

"A couple of kids wanted a student lounge.

"One student wanted a robot or computer to do his homework! (*Wait for laugh.*)

"But most of all, I learned that nearly all of you want more free time in school. You want more time to see your friends. A lot of you complained there's not enough time between classes to catch your breath, get your books, and get to the next class on time, let alone relax for a couple of minutes. Quite a few of you said that by the time you get through the lines in the cafeteria and eat your lunch, there's no time to talk.

"After hearing all this, I talked to a few people at other schools. I found out that at Spring Lane Middle School — right here in town — every student gets at least two free periods a week. Friends of mine in Harper's Ferry say they have an hour for lunch, which gives them plenty of time to hang out afterwards. In our local high school, students with a B+ average or better get all kinds of privileges.

"Finally, after thinking about what I learned, I decided I will bring up the following requests at the first Student Council meeting: (*Pause.*)

"I will ask to lengthen the lunch period to an hour.

"I will ask that every student gets at least two free periods a week. (*Raise two fingers for emphasis.*)

"I will ask that the time between classes be lengthened from three to five minutes. (*Raise three, then five fingers for emphasis.*)

"I will ask that students with a B+ average or better be given a free period instead of study hall every day. (*Pause.*)

"Wouldn't you like to increase your free time at school from two-and-a-half hours to six hours a week? As I have demonstrated, I have a realistic plan for giving you more free time. Elect me to the Student Council, and you will have time on your hands — free time!

"Once that goes through, I'll see about the student lounge!

"Thank you."

Wait up in front until the applause stops. After all, you've earned it for this speech and any other speech you prepare and deliver according to the steps in this book.

Speaker of the house

Big speeches like the ones shown in this book only come up once in a while. In between time, you can build up your speaker's confidence in other ways so that talking in front of people becomes something you do regularly and not just a couple of times a year. Here are a few parting tips to turn you into someone who enjoys talking before other people:

• Start noticing the speakers in your life like your teachers, the school principal, your minister, or rabbi. Which speakers always seem to get your attention? Notice the way these good speakers speak. Probably they talk about things you can relate to. They use a little humor to get you relaxed. They help you picture what they are talking about by giving good examples. They seem to be talking to *you* specifically because they take the trouble to mention experiences like those you may have had. They don't rush, yet they don't talk too long, either. Take a look at how these good speakers present themselves — the way they stand and dress, the way they use their voices and hands. Remember some of these details whenever you have to speak in front of people.

• Some kids are afraid of speaking in public and avoid it until they get a speech assignment. To lessen that fear, if you have it, take advantage of smaller speaking opportunities that come up every day. If you are prepared in your classes and know the right answers, raise your hand and share your information. You'll not only get quick practice in speaking before other people, you will probably boost your class grades, too. Try to think of one experience a day to share with your family at the dinner table. Or tell a joke if it's been a dull day. After you get used to doing this, try to present your experiences as stories with a beginning, middle, and end. After all, that's how you put a real speech together.

• Don't switch channels when politicians give speeches, press conferences, or debates. Politicians get professional advice on everything from what ties or scarves to wear to what jokes to tell. What makes you wish you could vote for some candidates and not for others? Is it what they are saying or *how* they are saying it?

• Everybody has something special they are interested in. When you have to give a talk about yourself, don't overlook the "little" subjects. Students have given talks on all sorts of things. Maybe you have a totally useless collection of business cards from stores, restaurants, and services all over town. You could give a terrific "travel" talk about your town just by talking about each place. Kids your age seem to hate wearing raincoats even when it's pouring. Why is this? Do you always order Sprite instead of 7-Up or Pepsi over Coke? A hamburger, never a hot dog? Why? How do you talk your way into getting money for something or getting out of doing chores around the house? You don't have to be presidential material to come up with good speaking topics. Whatever makes you *you* — your opinions, likes and dislikes, habits, and thoughts — that's what's worth talking about.

So don't grow up into one of those people who would rather meet a snake in the woods than talk to a group of people. You have some terrific things to talk about. Speak up!

Notes

Notes

Notes

Notes

Notes

Notes

Index

Appearance, 40, 46–47, 47–48, 61, 91–92, 95
Argument, 38–39
Audience, 6–7, 21, 23, 24, 28, 31, 33, 39, 47, 48, 49, 58, 77, 90

Body of speech, 26, 28, 29, 32, 33–34, 37, 42, 58, 73–74, 86

Campaign speeches, 50, 81–94
Closing sentences, 33, 58, 61, 74, 86
Comparisons, 36, 38–39, 60
Comparatives, 32
Conclusions, 26, 36–39, 42, 49–50, 58, 61, 75, 76, 77, 87, 88
Confidence, 40, 46–47, 47–48, 49–50, 61, 81, 91–92, 94, 95
Connectors, 32

Definitions, 36, 38
Delivering speeches, 46–50, 61, 77, 91–92
Demonstrations, 23, 24, 27, 56, 58, 63–64
Details, 26, 28, 33, 48, 95

Editing, 5, 25, 41–42, 61, 73–74, 76–77, 85–86, 88, 89
Entertaining speeches, 22, 27, 30–31
Examples, 28, 36, 39, 95
Eye contact, 44, 48, 50, 62, 77, 91

Gestures, 49

History speeches, 50, 66–80

How-to speeches, 22, 51–65

Informative speeches, 22, 51–65
Introductions, 26, 33, 34–36, 39, 41, 42, 43, 48, 58, 62,
    74, 75, 76, 87, 88, 91

Libraries, 11, 16–19, 67, 68

Main ideas, 26, 29
Memorizing, 36, 41, 42, 61, 88

Narrative speeches, 23, 66–80
Note cards, 2, 11–16, 18, 19, 20, 21, 24–31, 32, 36, 41,
    43, 46, 47, 54–56, 56–58, 61, 77, 83–85
  organization of, 12–16, 21, 24–25, 25–26, 27–28, 32,
      57–58, 73, 85–86
  preparation of, 28–29
Notes and note-taking: *see also* Note cards; 2, 4–5,
    11–16, 18, 19, 54–56, 69–72, 83–85

Opening sentences, 33, 36, 41, 58, 59–60, 61, 74, 86
Opinions, 35, 75–76, 89, 96
Order of a speech, 26–27, 61, 73
Organization
  of note cards, 12–16, 21, 24–25, 25–26, 27–28, 32,
      57–58, 73, 85–86
  of notes, 2

Pauses, 48, 49, 63, 64, 77, 78, 79, 91, 93, 94
Personal speeches, 50, 51–65
Personal stories, 28, 38, 60, 88, 95, 96
Persuasive speeches, 23, 27, 81–94
Practice, 3, 5, 31, 40–45, 61, 76–77, 88, 89, 90
Preparing

a campaign speech, 81–83, 83–85, 85–88, 88–90,
 90–91, 91–92
a history speech, 67–72, 73–74, 74–76, 76–77
a personal speech, 52–53, 53–56, 56–57, 57–58,
 58–60, 61–62
a speech, 2–3, 3–5, 5–10, 10–20, 21–24, 24–28,
 28–32, 33–40, 41–43, 43–45, 45–50
Props, 30, 45, 53

Questions
 in a speech, 37, 59, 75, 87
Quotations, 25, 26, 36, 38

Relaxing, 45–46, 47
Research, 4, 11, 16–19, 24, 29, 67–69, 69–72, 83–85

Schedules, 2, 3, 4–5, 52, 67, 81
Speeches: *see also* Delivering speeches; Note cards;
  Preparing; Schedules; Topics
 fear of giving, 1, 2, 4, 95
 kinds of, 22–23, 51–65, 66–80, 81–94
 length of, 3
 main idea of, 26, 29
 order of, 26–27, 61, 73
 parts of, 26, 28–29, 32, 33–39, 41, 43, 48, 49–50,
  59–60, 61, 62, 73–74, 75, 76, 77, 86, 87, 88, 91
 purpose of, 2, 21, 22, 23, 24, 25, 27, 56–57, 73, 85
Statistics, 33, 35, 38, 59, 87
Stories: *see* Personal stories
Subjects: *see* Topics
Summarizing, 39

Tape recording, 41, 45, 61, 89–90
Timing, 41, 42–43, 89–90

Topics, 2, 3, 5, 6–7, 7–9, 9–10, 11, 12, 16, 18, 19, 50, 52–53, 66, 67–68, 81–83, 96
  narrowing, 6–7, 9–10
  personalizing, 8–9, 9–10, 11, 12, 16, 95, 96

Visual aids, 17–18, 19–20, 26, 27, 28, 32, 33, 45, 46, 47, 49, 61, 62, 74, 77

Praise for
Sweet Georgia Brown

"Will keep you laughing and cheering for Georgia. It will evoke some teary eyes, but more than anything else, *Sweet Georgia Brown* will win your heart and soul."—Rawsistaz

"Robinson's writing is filled with humor and the revealing, touching moments of everyday life. Women everywhere will cheer."　　　　　　　　　　　—*Romantic Times*

"Fabulous. . . . Readers will appreciate this fine tale of transformation."　　　　　　　—*Midwest Book Review*

"What could have started out as a rags-to-riches story becomes a lot more complex as Robinson shows the other side of the riches, and that true happiness comes from the inside of the heart, not the inside of a bank."
　　　—Rachel Kramer Bussel, author of *He's on Top*

"*Sweet Georgia Brown* is a novel that will make women stand up and cheer." —Idrissa Ugdah, African American Literature Book Club

continued . . .

More Praise for the Novels of Cheryl Robinson

"A gifted writer, one of the best among contemporary African-American novelists."   —Book-Remarks.com

"A stunning character study."   —*Midwest Book Review*

"Laugh-out-loud snappy dialogue, compelling plot twists, and heart-feeling, genuine characters."   —Cydney Rax

"Fresh and exciting."   —*The Charlotte Post*

"A compelling read."   —Rawsistaz

"Had me spellbound."   —Nubian Sistas Book Club, Inc

"Cheryl Robinson . . . writes stories that entertain while giving the reader something to think about. Get lost in this complicated love story. You'll love it!"

—BlackLiterature.com